BY MY PRECISE HAIRCUT

Also by Cheryl Clarke:

BY
MY
PRECISE
HAIRCUT

Cheryl Clarke

The Hilary Tham Capital Collection
2016 Selections by Kimiko Hahn

THE WORD WORKS
WASHINGTON, D.C.

Cover art and design: Susan Pearce Design
Author photograph, front cover: Anne E. Chapman
Author photograph, back cover: Nívea Castro

ISBN: 978-0-944585-01-3
LCCN: 2015960105

acknowledgments

These poems have appeared, sometimes in slightly different versions, in the following publications:

Bloom: A Journal of Lesbian and Gay Writing: "Bald Woman"
Bone Bouquet: "Capital Car Chase"
The Wide Shore: "Oh Memory Fateful and Fatal" and "Sakia"
Feminist Wire: "One Million"
Long Shot: "A Sister's Lament"
Sinister Wisdom: "Songs of Longing"

"Body Double" was included in the anthology, *To Be Left with the Body*, publication of the AIDS Project, Los Angeles.

"A Sister's Lament" and "Please Read" appeared in *The Days of Good Looks: Prose and Poetry 1980-2005*.

All thanks to Julie R. Enszer and Esther Cohen for their unflinching feedback on this manuscript and to Nancy White for her thorough questions and wonderful energy.

contents

Dedicated to Miriam Carey,
Sandra Bland,
and all Black women
who have died unarmed at the hands of the state.

next (french film after the euro)

you kiss me deeply by ourselves and next
in front of me kiss your husband deep-
ly too for that stock tip. your tongue digs deep creep-

ing under on top diving swimming locking and
the acrid sweet of your spit. so deep next suction lock/auction
block   then the long trip (*voyage longue*)

down onto the Tunisian runner of bright coloration leg
resting on the rung of that squat leather tufted bar stool more
comfortable in romance than in the language of trade

and need next to someone so strung out and onto the vortex *em
seguida alors. alors* vex me. hex
me. *proteja-me* tongue me *c'est à qui* next

to each other (*sans mari*). no text like a tongue. only the text-
ure of tongues next tongues deep (*avec mari*).
em seguida. alors, alors. vex me. hex me.
proteja-me   tongue me   c'est à qui

reprise

for ginsberg: 1926-1997

sex
helped me through
no thanks to you
america

creeps me out sometimes too
loss of control
inevitability dark glasses lips parted
scarf cleavage
the right
tight
hip hang
of
it

histrionic clitoral ejaculation phallic thumb every chance we get
so long so far away and people over
the edge
america
like desire fresh and never never
wanting an end
even when the solo's too long
and too many chops already left out there
twitching

america
you've got a seized-up body that can't keep
your hands to yourself

so
there'd be the feel of her hairs
their surprise at my breath
the whistling tongue
pelvis-arcing ap
plauses
and wet
paus
es

V o l u p t u o u s n e s s
of muff moves against genital
moves

you

were nowhere near me that night
america
you
were breaking-in, raping,
taping, tapping, entrapping some
where on the other side of town
some
where.

one million

Black Women.
Nineteen-ninety-seven.
No mention
of HIV/AIDS.

elegy on 12 years a slave

Only screener.
Buy ticket and medium popcorn quick
from ticket-tenderer and her smartphone
in this pit of a strip mall matinee.
Lotta salt in large aluminum shakers
holes like dice pips.

No LED flashing in this pleat of a plex
and can't find *12 Years* cubicle.
Back to ticket-tenderer who escorts me
darkly, smartphone shoulder to ear.

Twelve Years a Slave: Solomon and Patsy
in Hollywood. East-West confluence.
Nigerian and Kenyan as platonic slaves.
(You don't have to *be* who you are to *play* who you are.
Remember Frank Silvera?)

Text to sprocket: a close reading.
Close-ups. Slow-moving. More plodding
than documentary. Reversals. Betrayals.
Dogged cruelty beyond my wildest metonyms.
Dogged resilience. Dogged survival.
Frailty. Fragility.

And still must endure Dred Scott, Reconstruction, Black
Codes, peonage, Jim Crow, lynch law, Plessy, segregation,
integration, stop and frisk, every shudder between
my thighs regarded.

No fiction, no exaggeration… But I forbear, Solomon attests.
Ear buds jacked to smartphone,
ticket-tenderer smiles and nods past my exit.

don't want to go

no farther back than
under the bed to look at moldy photo albums from the 30s
not the Gold nor Guinea Coast nor even Tulsa where
your nasty great-great-grandfather made a fortune
and lost it in that race riot.

No deed of an old maid slave mistress' whose
surname is spelled exactly like mine
or letters from a silly alcoholic birth father
or trading baseball cards with a sweet cousin half-sister.

No matricide or
murdered same-sex lover or
botched (secret) abortions
loud (secret) adoptions.

No accidental asphyxiation of a baby girl under
the drunken bodies of her loving parents.

those mammals: a cento of sorts

dancing feet paws or stout raked hooves
blush and split for us as revival as revealed
must crawl or be propelled or be brushed to their
seeming sleeping struck squash stuck poise   to the side
of the road
where a long time ago we had to grieve for them:
weep for them: pity them
but now my strange human duty makes me keep going even
if I know I swiped right down the middle of the white stripe
from head to tail of a greedy badger hovering at the perforated
median   its two halves creeping   to each its opposite side
to lie flat fur first to
the proximity of sky
the violence of spring
the lilac's knowledge
where the deer lives   and dies whining
and finally in silent prayerful fetal pose   at the edge

while only birds near escape collision except for the occasional
wild fowl foraging in twilight at the edge of a pasture of heifers
facing some rural route or the corpulent crow that won't leave
the fresh meat to the hawk on its way back to disembowel the
hen it scored in the first place
and it doesn't screech the broke-glass catastrophes of voice
the starlings have
as it backflips upon impact
          onto the strip of fresh asphalt leaving
its bloody blue-black plume fluttering   against
my driver's side windshield.

mandela: 12-5-2013

i.

Detroit journalist Marc Crawford introduced me to 'Nelson'
from a stack of circa 1970 Pathfinder Press pamphlets of his
pre-prison speeches in those days of intense indie publishing.

Then pointing to an oval-shaped, mahogany-colored object
with sprouts of white and dark hair—surely something's
hide—suspended on the back of his bathroom door, then
hefting the encumbrance to his shoulder, and then, like a comic
mimicking fucking thrusting it forward at me, Marc swore:

> 'I will be there with it when he gets free.
> This is his shield. He is Xhosa, you know.
> He gave it to me. Before Rivonia. To keep.
> I told him at his sentencing I would give it back
> to him when he's released.'

ii.

I read that pamphlet and memorized
Mandela's pie-shaped face,
off-center part in African hair,
and tribal leopard-skin cape
slung over his naked chest.

iii.

After the fall of Motown, wiry Willie Kgositsile
shouted through his broadsides,

'They used to call it Detroit!'

And that was forty years ago.
And that was yesterday.

a capital car chase

in memory of Miriam Carey, 1979-2013

Ah, if you would condone drone strikes
you would condone surveiling me here in little old
Stamford, Connecticut.

You finally got the starch to stand up to those Negro-hating
Republicans.

All those (white) patients I had to clean daily spying on me
through their implantology and root canals.

How sick I became looking in their mouths, especially as the
breath was usually foul. And especially if they asked what kind of
degree I have—code for was I skilled enough to be looking down
their fetid throats—and 'who takes care of your daughter while
you work?' and 'what does your husband do?'

All that would be enough to send anybody careening onto
1600 Pennsylvania Avenue in a late model Infiniti. No car
lasts forever. But my daughter survived in that luxury-car
baby car-seat, poor little orphan. NY child services says
she's fine, though. Imagine how my family will have to spin
my 'wrongful death' to her.

Ah, I shall not speculate on the obvious.

I drove to 1600 Pennsylvania Avenue unarmed, because I
heard his droning voice telling me he couldn't do anything
about the voices luring me to Federal Triangle that day.

Why, he even monitored my funeral.

'Did they really have to shoot her to death? Hunh? Just post-partum depression with a little psychosis,' *chirps my tearful sister.*

(Couldn't none of you all speak up before? Break the silence? Why do black people always have to be at the proverbial end of a frayed rope before anyone declares, 'You are crazy.')

Ah, how that ammo hurt—but not for long.
Ah, and how invisible I still was to the Hill that never noticed my demise.

'Did I have to lose a sister?'

You still asking that, Sis?

'Couldn't they have shot her tires?'

Are you kidding, Sis? Cops can't shoot that straight.

'She was unarmed,' *Mama cries.*

Coulda been a car bomb in my baby car seat instead of your granddaughter, Mama! Ah, too little too late, Mama?

They had to aim for the overkill. Remember Amadou?
41 shots later and all he had was a billfold.

imagine

Just you girls—you and four-month-old Zanaiah—
off to your favorite mall to buy little after-xmas knickknacks
for forgotten relatives, but mainly to get out, see some life
again, and show Zee off: prettiest little brown dimpled rascal
in her yellow and green snow suit from Auntie Toby.

Some more. You drive up to the half full parking lot thinking
about how Zee's daddy couldn't get over how you don't want
him to move in. 'How I'm gonna know my girl is being
taken care of if I'm not here taking care—of both my girls,'
he condescended as he proffered the baby tote.

Some more. You're walking inside thinking to your 30-
something self with Zee in tote as the baby carriages of 15-
something gum-chewing, texting moms glide by cursing
their phones, each other, and their baby daddies.
You smile as you imagine college for Zee, if not private
primary and secondary. Already a Baby Einstein DVD set.

You are moving on into Stride Right, your fave shoe store.
You set Zee down in her tote
to peruse the latest offerings in size 11—no size 11s.
Two minutes at most you turn back to Zee—
no tote.

You shriek staccato, 'My baby! My baby! She's… gone!
Gone! Gone, gone.'
Some customers irked, their consuming frenzies forestalled.
Some fearing drugs, hunger or homelessness till they glance
askance at your custom suede coat.
Some in blind empathy.

The store manager calls someone who gives you a bottle of
really cold water and helps you sit on the low chair,
the lock-down in progress.

You must call Zee's daddy away from his monitor and other
people's money (his own too) and your girlfriend from her
smart car and, no, you do
not call your mother or your father—yet.

An hour. Baby Zee in one's arms and her baby tote slung over
the other's, police duo explains:
'We have her in custody, ma'am. She stole your baby,' says one,
flashing his badge at your nose.
'Kidnapped,' you correct.
'She wanted to prove to her boyfriend she had his baby in
hopes he would marry her. What advice can I give you, ma'am,
except to never take your eye off your baby.'

You scratch the air above their advice to wrest free
the unflappable Zee, the hood of Auntie Toby's snow suit and
her tote pendulous:

'Is it *all* and *only* on my eye?' you query.

women of letters

i.

Belinda's Petition Remembered

I was stolen.

Seventy years toiling this side of the sea, verdant
forests, mountains, seasons of color, heat, and the ruthless cold.
Odd creatures. Never a moment to myself, honorable
sirs. We are suing. Seventy years and am I not less than a slave
that I cannot protect myself from the betrayal of abandonment
by who called himself my master, a loyalist fleeing, leaving me
and my infirm daughter to dwell in penury? We are suing.

(You, sirs, perhaps may imagine the rigors of that voyage.
300 Africans. I lay above deck between two women not of my
language chained to one another by the ankles. Our doom
slavery. We were separated in Tobago. A young girl made to lay
me between her nubile breasts to Virginia but was not able to
fight off the abominators, escaping overboard their hairs and
smells.)

We are suing.

ii.

PLEASE READ

Pulaski, Tenn., July 15, 1883

DEAR FRIENDS:

*I am trying to find out where my children are.
Please help me. Their names are Diana, Henry, Drucilla
and George Washington. Before the war we belonged to
Mr. W. M. Thompson, in Rutherford County, North Carolina.
About thirty years ago, after the death of our old Mistress,
Diana and Drucilla were taken from me and carried into
Georgia. George Washington was taken away from Jackson
County, Alabama, by the soldiers during the war.*

*I, their mother, was Hannah Thompson, but have since
married a man named Powers. Please read this notice in the
churches, and anyone knowing of my children will confer a favor
by writing to me.*

Address,
HANNAH POWERS,
   Pulaski, Tennessee.

iii.

Letter from a close friend
written four days after you die and received
three days after your birthday

April 22, 1967
905 4 Ave So apt 1
Great Fall Mont
738 Madison St. N.W.
Wash. D.C.

Hi Hannah.

Just a few lines to let you here from me the reason I
am so long writing you is because I have had the flue again
and still cant shake it off I still have it but not as bad as at
first I just ant felt like writing or doeing nothing Just do fix
my food when I get like this it leave me weak and the days is
so so long out here. And the nights to I have a lot of friends
but still get lonesome here for home so I will try to get home in
July if I dont have no more sickness but I have spent a lot
of money for sickness. So I will trust in God and he will help
me. I eat just what I wont and any time I think about
cornbread and greens I think about you and cooking
chitlings for Friday and Sat. if the Lord spears me. I have
sent Bertha cards and a letter and she still don't write so I
ant going to write her no more. Do Mildred still live where
she did and what have become of Marion and May and Anna
Perry. I sure hope all that old bunch will be living when I get

home it is snowing like mad now will write more next time
and wont be so long answering.

Give all your family my love.

From a friend
Geraldine

All ways glad to here from you.

the (only) athlete

Jack
Roosevelt
Robinson, 'Jackie,'
1947, integrated   white
baseball a portion of the game
devoted to controlling   himself:
grandson of a slave   the Negro   Leagues
overqualified Branch an experiment: insults,
loneliness, abuse 'hey boy, come pick my cotton.'
tensions high   Rachel in the stands rooting (Rachel
always rooting) Pee Wee 29 stolen bases the death
of the   Negro Leagues   star of his own bio pic.

Ja

ck

ie

C a m p a i g n i n g for Nixon in 1960.
Derided by Malcolm X as a 'Tom.'
The death of J a c k i e J r.
Did he really do more for
the Negro than Martin
Luther King Jr? Did
Malcolm X real
ly read *Uncle*
Tom's
Cab
i
n?

oh memory fateful and fatal

i. elegy for 1963

how many anniversaries can anyone accommodate in one
year not to live in anticipation of events to become next year's
celebrations and memorializations?

Jackson, Mississippi: 'NAACP Field Secretary Medgar Evers
Shot' in the back getting out of his car in front of his house and
strong man that he is, drags himself up by the car door handle,
staggering up the steps, collapsing on his front porch as Mrs.
Evers, the three little Evers, and awakened neighbors look on
hysterically, one firing a shot to scare off the assassin.

Washington, D.C.: our neighbor, recent widow Mrs. Flowers,
joins us full of hope as we ride the bus to the Lincoln Memorial
on that hot August day for 'Jobs and Freedom,' returning
to watch 'I Have a Dream' on television. Tipped off by FBI,
Maryland State Police turn back Klansmen just outside
the District line, carful of weapons.

Birmingham, Alabama: when Mrs. Davis, a neighbor, drives
a frantic Mrs. Robertson to the 16th Street Baptist Church
where the dynamite detonated into the basement choir prac-
tice, Mrs. Robertson's father breaks the news of her daughter
Carole's murder, 'She's gone, baby.'

Dallas, Texas: asked by an aide if she would like to 'clean up'
from the blood, Mrs. Kennedy advises, 'Let them see
what they have done.'

ii. zapruder

i google-hunt that zapruder film on youtube enhanced with
color and slow-mo and pant for the frames where jack thinking
to smooth his hair back from his face instead surprised grips
his hand over his forehead and the other over his throat as the
first bullet enters and exits and turning to jackie falls over on
her shoulder as the second shot tears into that cool hyannis-
bred brain and jackie in her white kid gloves chases that
brahmin brain as it is jettisoned out onto the deck of that sleek
61 lincoln before the secret service forces her back by jack's
fallen side while the rest of us take cover in front of monitors
and on the lawn across the street from that texas schoolbook
depository and wonder if a third or fourth shot was fired and
all those years we thought cynically jackie was trying to escape
out of the back of that fully-loaded presidential continental for
as she told her maid the next day 'i thought they might've killed
me too.'

bald woman

Grown bald in a place hidden from ordinary sight—
except mine—and
held in memory most of the time.

I ask my lover if she is losing hers?
And sleepily I grab at her crotch. Dodging my hand,
she laughs, kisses me 'nightee-night' and climbs gingerly
the three flights to bed.

You always knew you'd be stuck downstairs resenting
changes, comparing them to others like your lover's the same age
and wondering *do I look like I'm bald in a place*
I once could run your fingers through.

It set me apart.

a sister's lament as she poses
for an AP photograph
holding her dead sister's portrait

Black women are accustomed to being firsts, and here you go
being first again:

Sgt. J. L. Winters,

'first [African] American [u.s.]/[black] servicewoman [of
mixed ancestry] to die since the war [against/with
Afghanistan] began.'

Says our family friend, Ron:
'The price we have to pay for what happened on 9-11.'

Why? Is your body to be bartered, levied, or charged?
Does he know it was priceless and peerless and that you knew
what you were stepping to?

And here I stand
for the public
holding this picture of you in your uniform
(looking so pretty in it)
and your eyes aren't convinced
or resigned
to being 'the price.'
Nor are mine.

We look eerily identical
but opposite.
I'm dressed in jeans, tee shirt, and parka.
I don't half-smile or look into the camera with old glory
displayed behind me.

I fairly suck my teeth and stare piss-faced
askance with a suburban chimney as backdrop.

I look like a ventriloquist
holding this portrait instead of you in my arms.

I'm lonely as a convict out here outside of Gary
while you are crashed into a mountainside in Pakistan.

A mysterious mistake.
Not 'hostile fire,' say the secretaries
and generals.
Were you thinking it'd end this soon?
We look eerily identical.

songs of longing

for Sandra Rattley

i. rainbow at the Regal '65

There's a rainbow
i-in my heart tha-at
reminds me-ee of
of how we pa-ar-ted....
My love is gone forever.
But deep down in my heart,
I'll love her forever....

Screeching 'rainbow'
screams of fantasy seekers
vying with the precise insistence of a favorite falsetto.

> *Whatever   it   is   the rainbow*
> *is never enough*
> *even when the suicide is*
> *so well-planned.*
> *The superintendent reads who to contact*
> *to take the body down*
> *and damn you for tying that slip knot so expertly.*

High pitched swoons.
Homage at the Regal.
One mo' chance
The lonely duke, duke, duke, duke
of Chicago.

Oh Chi'.

ii. South East (S.E.)

Like Marvin
I used to be too nervous
to party.
We're from the
same town
but he grew up
in South East
a shanty town
of jacklegs like his father ('Father')
who beat the boy Marvin after making him strip
naked almost every day
and killed him in a coke rage
(Marvin that is) almost 40 years later.
'C'était tragique'
a Parisian tabloid quoted
a Motown spokesperson
in L.A.

That's what we still think about
that rough trash in South East (S.E.).
Not like us farther *in* in North East (N.E.)
more than a decade later in our
segregated developments beginning
that long lateral stride into the North West (N.W.)
and the lower middle class.

iii. 2007

for the big o
loving you forty years late
loving mucus stockpiling in your throat
loving that relentless climax
who will sing to us since your passion died?
who will sing passion to us?
who will sing?

iv. ice man

Broken up blues hymn
between my synapses:
deeper and wider than any
sho nuff sea

Broken up blues hymn
panting between your rayon slacks
my back against the wall of frequency
wanting

Broken up blues hymn
twanging signals
VeeJay amp   velvet larynx
satin tux   suede dress pumps

that *je ne sais quoi* soul
Broken up blues hymn
muted grief of women
uncertain of what tomorrow brings

Don't try to spare my feelings.
Just tell me that we're through.

v. falsetto

if r&b songs of unrequited love are channeling ex-slaves'
sadness hurt disappointment and pissed hostility at white
america's dastardly treatment of them and everybody else's
asses darker than a whiter shade of pale but especially
niggers' asses;
then the tight pants patent leather loafers (no dime) green-eyes
hair laid all the way to sunday morning miracle mulatto
falsetto boy was the deepest exponent of
ooh, ooh, ooh,
oh, oh, oh,
woo, hoo, ooh
baby baby.

vi. coda

parlor dance party with an i-pod of 5000 songs only as far
back as charles brown. sandy my oldest friend a good dancer
since junior high school to come bop with me and pony
across some linoleum or hard wood & long for my mother
(who surveilled me slow drag with a mustachioed boy named
james a smooth caramel baritone year older—and shy). yes,
do that party and reprise those gritty songs that fed and
desegregated the soul. yes, do it with some rhythm. moreso
some substances. all those dumped cadavers. yeah. all that
studio work and live shows and riots. and y'all dead. hey,
y'all dead. comin' home. back in my (project) arms again.
heroin. cancer. and grits. a party like grits. yeah. come and
git it. left sitting on the dock and rock was reprising what we
knew already. gimme that baby sound falsetto aching tenor
that passion and phlegm: *shame on me shame on me I made
a big mistake when I see my babe again I'm gonna bake me a
cherry cake 10 thousand dollar reward for the first one who find
her when I git my hands on her I'm gonna just chain and bind
her.* a need-tuh-need-yuh-baby sound to dance party to.

like the 45 the c.d. is over no matter the extra takes and still
yearning for when dancing was the life the stomp slop cha
cha cha tighten up the steps and turns and holding and
cradling arms and longing on linoleum and hardwood till
school or mule intervention.

block elder

My Father was a block elder. Like my younger sisters
and me, all the children and their parents on the block
called him Pop-Pop.

Worked at midnight, watched us and everybody else's
children in the daytime, walked us to and from school.
Was welcomed and unthreatened in the company of
neighbor women.

When Pop-Pop and my previously married Mother bought
that '51 Dodge in '55 with bonds she'd saved, he drove us all
across town. Smoked Chesterfields and cursed sparingly.

Before he was Pop-Pop, he was gray-haired, even as he left
for the war in 1941—the only unmarried son. His own
mother could not leave work before he had to get his bus
for camp. So she fried him chicken. His younger sister's
sassy daughter cried, 'unka, unka' after him and clung to his
leg, and even my mother's 2 waif-like children, living
across the street with their mean grandmother, begged him
from the sidewalk to come back before dusk, as he bent
the block to Liverpool and the Luftwaffe.

Pop-Pop returned in '45 in time to meet his mother strolling
from work up that fabled block of 4-story row houses their
family had owned for a generation. As always, she'd changed
from her green and white char dress to her flowered street
clothes and hose for the walk home. She ran to him, casting
down her pocketbook
        and even her
                shopping bag
                        spilling its soiled articles.

My Father was a block elder and the children
flocked to him for band-aids and wagon rides.
He glued toys and patched bike tires. Teenagers
came to him for car rides and driving lessons.

Our neighbor was like a fourth sister to us and daughter
to Pop-Pop. Her own parents, lawyers, believed in afternoon
cocktails, in which she shared. After we left the block, she
stayed on to care for her father when her mother died of
cancer. Refused to finish high school. Years later, debilitated
from bourbon and brandy and caring for her father, she came
running to Pop-Pop ragged-clad calling him 'Mr. _____ '
(instead of the familiar) to signal her seriousness.

Pop-Pop was a block elder and listened to her confession
of transgression against her father. Swore Pop-Pop to secrecy
even from us, especially from us, and he took the secret to
his grave though we had long since discerned the transgression
and it was not hers. She died nearly homeless. With her
confession behind his lips, Pop-Pop died soon after, alone
but comforted. He was a block elder.

the empire

you built, Ruth
on that red and black label
        spin
    ning
        that
skinny spindle of rhythm and
  commerce for Ertegun, the Mardin brothers
  and Wexler.
   25
    years later: making
   your comeback wanting
  to listen to your
 old 'stuff.' Discovering 'So Long' on 78
dustjacket intact $100 in a L.A. record shop
  made you really pissed over those $69 royalty
   checks for the music you made.
  Inventress of the hoochie
   coochie. Whacking that tambourine on your
    crinoline backside. Fanning your own lovely bosom.
    Making white mothers wanna
   keep their sons at home, white fathers wanna treat
  their daughters mean.

some dead

Negro
Jew
Muslim matron gang-raped
homosexual girl named 'Gift' wire-strangled
naked orthodox woman forced through a gauntlet of carbon
monoxide
black teenaged city boy dredged from a rural river
still
haunt the living
no matter uncovering mass graves, dredging rivers,
claiming bodies, body parts, rings, scarves, wigs, toys

perpetual anniversary recitations of numbers and names.

Some dead
Negro
Jew
Muslim matron gang-raped
Homosexual girl wire-strangled
naked orthodox woman gassed
sassy black teenaged boy's body mangled
still
haunt the living
no matter.

d.c. meditations

i. post-post reconstruction

Washington. Detroit. Rutherfordton. Bloody Tulsa Pearl left
the red dust of serfdom to the mean old black man who
named her.

Willy had that tincture of the African, white-skinned like
his mother.

The whole family was evicted when the landlord, thinking
Willy white, later saw Pearl and her dusky children.

She followed him to work and met him coming home in later
years to ensure he wasn't passing. Allowed a mania about
the downstairs neighbor trying to seduce him.

That was later. Years of bed confusion, loneliness, despair—
later.

Far from the days of good looks.

ii. Washington

Nineteen fifty-four, playing piano at graduation in
segregated Dunbar high school sweet loam of its fragile black
bourgeoisie.

Nineteen fifty-nine, knives drawn over the desegregation of
the whites-only amusement park in Glen Echo, Md.

iii. tines in the road

Paul Laurence Dunbar battered Alice Moore Dunbar
and walked through LeDroit Park occasionally.
Duke Ellington painted signs
and marveled at the stride of James P. Johnson.
Alain Locke went to Paris.
Mary Church Terrell organized sit-ins.

iv. Brevard

walked on the balls of his feet, especially when let outta jail
after behaving disorderly. Hannah, his wife, had him locked up,
fanning herself on the front porch watching him approach in
his rakish bowler.

Brevard was beloved of Edna, in that 1920 tintype, recently
discovered among Hannah's keepsakes after Edna's death.
Edna—aged 4 astride Brevard's motorcycle frowning into the
camera while three other men laugh into the lens. Brevard
astride behind Edna holding her on the seat her hair loose
from its plaits, unkempt—shamed her in later years. And
made me wonder today, like Alice Walker, about a little girl
around a yard full of grown men, even her beloved cousin
among them and no woman in sight unless behind the box.

v. epiphany 1924

the head altar boy:
at holy savior, the first catholic church founded by Blacks
over there on the treacherous part of the river.
father shane in the sacristy passes
him the roman chalice filled with leftover wafers to store
fondles him.

vi. Shenette S. Brown, 1999 graduate of Edward
Kennedy Ellington High School on what she learned

'Everything's gotta be right
and tight
and outta sight.'

vii. may day

Should we celebrate the fall
of the Berlin Wall
or mourn the failures of democracy?
To think Marian Anderson may be more remembered for
singing to 75,000 people in front of the 'Great Emancipator's'
sculpture in Jim Crow D.C. after being
refused Constitution Hall by the D.A.R.

Instead of for that stunning voice—at turns deep, clear, muddy,
atonal, bell-like
almost flat sometimes with the guttural longing
of 'Deep River'
and the loneliness of separate dining.

in this hostile corridor

A quickening
nostalgia suffuses
me this late evening

fin de siècle
between
two endangered sites.

The marvelous
have been blighted
by a blood-borne

scourge. Flamboyantly frail
pretty   still marvelous   you
nourish our failing geographies.

Am dazzled as I face your solicitousness
over the counter of this nasty
KFC:

your articulated brows
mascara the discrete texture
of your facial skin and buffed cultivated nails.

You recognize
me too—
by my precise haircut.

a child die

for Amina Baraka

i. Shani Baraka and Rayshon Holmes

Reticent naming is not witness enough.

I went to that courtroom in New Jersey to see Ibn Pasha,
domestic abuser and killer of 'hard-loving black women,'
Shani Baraka and Rayshon Holmes, Shani's 'companion.'
Estranged mate of Shani's older sister. Skinny, nerdy, color
of a walnut shell, innocuous-looking in Buddy Holly frames
killer.

(So unlike the stern, serious revolutionaries Sundiata Acoli
and Assata Shakur in that same courtroom where I surveilled
injustice daily 38 years ago.)

After sneaking back to the house to further harm his wife,
instead, he shot you and Rayshon in the head and body
multiple times. Stole your watch, gift from 'Ray,' pawned it
in Baltimore.

Reticent naming is not witness enough.

28 years ago I wrote a baleful poem to your aunt—Kimako
Baraka/Sondra Elaine Jones—also a 'hard-loving' (woman-
loving) black woman, also murdered by a misguided man
who also stole her jewelry. Put up so tough a fight, he had to
stab her in the head and body multiple times.

Reticent naming is not witness enough.

ii. Kyra Mills

(posted with photo on a mailbox at 14th St. and 6th Ave.,
New York City, fall 2001.)

6 years old

last seen hold-

ing her mother's hand

on the 92nd floor of Tower One.

iii. à Jacqueline

(Haiti, January 30, 2010)

Jacqueline, 10 years old, 10 feet under 5 feet of concrete, her
classmate lying near. Chris, her rescuer and a missionary
from the States, only had a hammer. He needed help.
Jacqueline had been praying for hours—for herself, her
classmate lying near, and for Chris. So had Chris. He knew
the classmate was dead. He stopped digging as afternoon
gave way to twilight.

*I will be back. I must get help. It is getting dark. I need light and
help and more tools. I will be back. Pray. Pray.*

He walked four miles to get a bus.

The bus took four hours to get to my house....

*Drive back in the morning. Race to where I had last held her
prayers in my ears, the cinder block and concrete burial
ground the school had become. Jacqueline was dead—how could a
child die? Would she have held on if she knew I would be back in
the morning. I mean, if I had said it. If I had said,
"I will be back in the morning." This will haunt me
for more than a while.*

iv. Sakia (1987-2003)

Hey, girl, I want you to know.
I'm gonna miss you so much if you go.

Thought your 'AGgressive' truth could stop that reckless mouth
battering us all our black woman lives? He is in jail for 25 years
with the specter of that knife he stabbed into your fearless
fifteen- almost sixteen-year-old chest one early mo/urning at a
Newark (N.J.) bus stop on Broad and Market.

Let us mark
the bloody space of your martyrdom
your no-place-to-be-who-you-were
our collusion.

v. temporal zone

for Najeeb, b. 1974

Since 1989, will keep on writing this elegy, when you fell,
strangely, and we were locked in the danse sepulchral of that
temporal zone as you lay dying for 18 hours. 'I don't want him
uncovered in the middle of the ward. It's so cold out there,'
your mother tells the young head nurse capable and loving
patting a sick baby on her chest making her rounds and calls
giving injections and intravenouses. Residents hover, begging
measurements.

Leave ward the zone hanging heavy. Sleep fuck get drunk or
high for 4 hours. 'There is no brain activity.' To lose the body
so quick. Before your grandparents arrive to lay on hands. And
when they arrive do not resist the hands they lay on us and
listen to old, old anecdotes. New stories from our father of
how he drove with no brakes in a supply convoy on Normandy
Beach a day after D-Day, remembering his Sergeant's words: 'A
job only a nigger would be given to do.' He laughs and is tearful
over the ironies of dying.

We think of your mangled face and spleen. 'He had such a
strong, strong heart,' our mother says.

Neighbors close friends ex-lovers ex-husbands step into
the zone. One beauteous mauve-skinned woman, your
classmate's mother, vivid lipstick, recounts that her elegant
bachelor uncle loved gin and vermouth straight up in that
pyramidal crystal as I drain mine to the base of its vertex
talking louder after each swallow and thinking jealously,

'At least you still have your child.' The enchanting deep hollow of her cleavage shames my low impulse.

We choose the urn.

A warped hymn strains from the fire escape:

> *But will my heart be broken*
> *when the night meets the morning sun?*

vi. 'failure nor success is ever final'

If not a brave puppeteer and member of the drama club a good soloist a behind the scenes class president twice and class sweetheart and not also a member of the honor society and her whole future before her—we might not have known about this horror in Milford, Ct. where they think it's another world and safe for children but it's not—like, remember Sandy Hook? Same old world of white male presumptuous and privileged desire: dark depressed tuned-out turned down and needing reassurance. And surely a girl with the last name Sanchez should want to reassure him a friend since middle school.

Stabbed her in the neck. In the hallway of John Law High School—'Law'? This not a sonnet. Bled to death in front of teachers librarians staff in the Math wing where they think it's another world and safe for children but it's not—like, remember Sandy Hook—the same old world of white male presumptuous and privileged desire: dark depressed tuned out turned down and needing reassurance in front of teachers librarians and staff. A friend since middle school. This is not a sonnet.

Think of how safe her family thought she'd be when she left out for school that early morning six days after the Resurrection.

A brave puppeteer.

not the only

9-11:

Chile. 1971. CIA coup d'état.
Suicide. Murder. Rape.
Arena of torture.

Survivors of Pinochet
clanging pots and pans
to shame his atrocities.

Never enough clanging.
Never enough shaming.

my brother needs at least

a poem:
Queer small swimmer painter pianist
coulda been a winner
in another time
another father
another mother (my mother too) tried and acquitted of
homicide and later remarried.
Expected you to get a job in the gov't
whatever else you did with
your excessive gifts.
You chose air force—error.
Discharged and trained as a draftsman. Dried your soul.
29 years at the Pentagon, witnessed in '59 the loss to fire of the
'secret data,' not a day without vodka.
Dead from its ravages
queer small swimmer painter pianist
with your military so-long-salute somewhere in Virginia.
Your butch colleague
her uncomfortable skirt and wooden shoes
—a heart-wringing eulogy.
Two sisters offer more oblique praise.
The two of us suppressed any funereal corniness.
Mother hid her blindness behind the usual glamour.
For the second time I met your daughter, painter and singer,
dying of lupus, holding your flag to her breast. Her own
daughter shipping to Afghanistan in August.

racing terror

for Katrina survivors

i. high dive

i'm glad my mother died two years before this mess or she
mighta been one of those old old women trapped by the water
as it swole up to the
3rd
4th
5th floor
& she couldn't git out & she drown-ded remembering
her salad days on the high dive six years after
the great flood of '27.

as it was she died of congestive heart failure a drowning of
another sort.

she went down hard cursing us all for not rescuing her
from the end.

ii. new deal to raw deal

detroit was hard in 1943
with white migrant attacks on black migrant paradise valley.
roosevelt's way to deal with the dixiecrats.
huac.
federal fair employment practices.
integration of the army.
mccarran.
mccarthy.
martyrdom of malcolm x.
murder of martin king:
memphis, oh, memphis.
COINTELPRO.
1973:
blood and
BLA stencils dot a trail along the n.j. turnpike
up to welfare reform.
patriot act.
levies breeched.

iii. 'only whites need relocate to mississippi'

'browner' called you all day long to tell you the category 5
was gonna wash the crescent away.

won't listen. can't listen. don't wanna listen. nothing and
nothing will stop oil-rich dixiecrat texans who won't relocate
to oil-rich nigeria

and ray nagin

crying from a holiday inn.

'only whites need relocate to mississisppi (*or* washington, d.c.,
for that matter).'

iv. 'there ain' no place fo' a po' ol' gal to go'

don't nobody care what happen to no negroes, notoriously not
poor ones with nappy hair and bad cholesterol cursing the
government from the superdome or floating atop the flood
waters of the ninth ward. (ones—so unlike oprah winfrey—
whose feet barbara bush do not want on her coffee table either,
nor do oprah. but those 'feet hurt like nobody's business.')

we knew them way before katrina. just like those iraqi so-called
insurgents creeped up into the middle of wmd lies katrina
busted those levies.

lies, levies, and prescription/prescripting drug fiascos.

'what?! what?! medicaid won't cover my diabetes medicines
no' mo'! well, scarlet, you can just pull that $200 out yo' ass. i'm
gon' go git me some other use outta these syringes and git it all
ovah with before that bird flu git here.

no quarantine for me. terrorists take me to hell.'

iv. 2005 delaware county to the parish of orleans

a thousand miles north
we pass a beauteous cemetery.
stones old as 1803.
diminutive stones for:

        2   3   4   5   6

children
dead at 10 weeks to 13 years.
      the great blue heron lands on a marshy field
    and takes off immediately arcing its neck.
        we follow the sound of its wings
          under a 21 foot high
          wall of water
        to other graves above
      ground then to rampart street
    alighting
   atop
a mule-drawn pyre
   fugitives and orphans
   march shoulder to
   shoulder to claim
   and rename
   congo square

working my way

back
to
Billie Holiday.
     arriving
redolent.
such a pretty
back
to old justifications:

     butch-femme

     s-m

maitresse   ou   esclave

vanilla   chocolate   strawberry

throat deep
right to my ears.

19 lines for easter 2014

Dead voices these late March days sing to me
round that old wood stove with a half century
of songs re-recorded on compact disk (no warmth but at
least no surface noise). Fetal season ambivalent about the
coming hosannas crueler than April. Fetid snow stockpiled with
fall leaves. Litter in relief. Dead voices these late March days
and my late aunt (all my aunts are late now) loved that nasal
voice and schoolboy face and the legend of a chick swinging
on one arm and his trumpet snuggled under the other. Yes,
burning the book at both ends. On the stand, beyond the stage
door, down the alley smack, always smack, years before
he cast himself (or was cast) gargoyle-faced and snaggle-
toothed from a balcony in Amsterdam in the middle of a really
good comeback and a dope deal gone bad. My late aunt
still loved the legend of that burnt book. Reprised it every
time she spun one of his hyperbolic love lyrics. Voice and
trumpet still sweet, though no teeth to enunciate either.

…There is no night. There is no day.

wings

Sex waits in the wings, second, third,
or tenth after writing. 'Sex disturbs too much
when you're older and haven't had it in more
than ten years. Bergman only invented it
for the 60s generation,' quips a friend
who moved to Stockholm.
Writing is so much is waiting for conceits
exquisite intimate sudden surprising familiar.
With your left hand clasp your left breast.
Catch your breath.
Promise yourself to practice.

notes

The poem "One Million" is dedicated to the copy-cat
One Million Black Women's March which took place in
Philadelphia in October of 1997. I found it odd that a call
upon one million black women to assemble included no
prominence given to AIDS, the number one cause of mortality,
at that time, for black women between the ages of 18 and 44.
According to the Centers for Disease Control and Prevention
on a page last updated in February, 2016, "Blacks/African
Americans have the most severe burden of HIV of all racial/
ethnic groups in the United States. Compared with other
races and ethnicities, African Americans account for a higher
proportion of new HIV diagnoses, those living with HIV, and
those ever diagnosed with AIDS." <www.cdc.gov/hiv/group/
racialethnic/africanamericans/index.html>

"Elegy on *12 Years a Slave*": The passage, "This is no fiction, no
exaggeration.... But I forbear..." is taken from the last chapter
of Solomon Northup's narrative, originally entitled *Twelve Years
a Slave, Narrative of Solomon Northup, a Citizen of New York,
Kidnapped in Washington City in 1841, and Rescued in 1853,
from a Cotton Plantation Near the Red River In Louisiana*. It was
first published in 1853 (Louisiana University Press, 1968).

"Some Dead." Baby Suggs in Toni Morrison's *Beloved* says, "Not
a house in the country ain't packed to its rafters with some
dead negro's grief," signifying we are never free of the massacred
bodies that sanctify our lands. The screams of all our murdered
dead haunt us: from the bottom of the Atlantic Ocean, to the
"bloodlands" of Eastern Europe and Russia, to the homophobic
streets the world over.

In "A Capital Car Chase," the dedication to Miriam Carey refers to the 34-year-old dental hygienist and mother who drove her car, a black Infiniti, through the police barricades and onto the grounds of the White House on October 3, 2013. The secret service ordered her to stop and she continued driving at high speeds through downtown D.C. traffic toward the Capitol grounds where she was finally stopped after driving into oncoming traffic, striking another off-duty secret service vehicle en route to the Capitol grounds, then backing up into another vehicle. She was shot five times in the back. She died. Miraculously, her one-year-old daughter survived. Her family has filed a wrongful death suit, after the U.S. Attorney for Washington, D.C., found that excessive force was not used. I guess we all remember the man from Texas who in 2014 was able to climb a fence in front of the White House and enter the front door concealing a knife, who was merely arrested.

"A Cento of Sorts" includes lines from Jake Adam York's "Small Birds of Sound" in *Murmuration of Starlings*; Bertha Rogers' "IV. March" in *Even the Hemlock*; Marilyn Hacker's "Letter on June 15" in *Winter Numbers*; Eavan Boland's "Elegy for My Mother in Which She Barely Appears"; my own "Jazz Poem for Morristown NJ"; Harmony Holiday's "Motown Philly Back Again"; and Gerald Stern's "Writing Like a Jew."

"Mandela." Marc Crawford (1929-1996) was a journalist for *Ebony, Jet, Life, Encore*, and *Freedomways*. He covered very dangerous civil rights struggles, was arrested and kicked in the teeth. Of course Mandela was in jail for life at the time I knew Marc in the early 1970s as an instructor at Livingston College in New Brunswick, N.J. I don't know if he made it to Mandela's release in 1990. Marc was a really wild man. Keorapetse W. Kgositsile (b. 1938) was a South African poet and political activist and influential member of the ANC, who was in exile in U.S 1962-1975 and joined the Black Arts

Movement. Sometimes called "Willie," he published poetry
with Broadside Press, the major independent press propagating
the poetry of the movement. Broadside was located in Detroit.

"Women of Letters: ii. Belinda's Words Remembered."
Belinda, a slave in the Royall House, wrote a petition to the
Commonwealth of Massachusetts in 1783, requesting an
income from the estate of her former owner, Isaac Royall. See
also Rita Dove's poem, "Belinda's Petition." Section iii., "Letter
from a close friend written four days after you die and received
three days after your birthday," is in memory of my aunt,
Hannah T. Logan 10-23-1894 – 4-18-1967.

"Racing Terror" is dedicated to the survivors of the 2005
hurricane, Katrina, which nearly destroyed New Orleans. I was
in Delaware County, N.Y. when it was ravaging the Big Easy.
The Bush Administration was ready to let the city die. Bush
flew over the city once and never visited its inhabitants, many
of whom were displaced to other states, rather like refugees
with not much assistance from the state or federal governments
to relocate. See the documentary, *Getting Back to Abnormal*,
about post-Katrina New Orleans, by Louis Alvarez, Andrew
Kolker, Peter Odabashian, and Paul Stekler.

In section ii. "new deal to raw deal," I allude to the ghastly
1943 Detroit race riot. Only lasting two or three days, this
race riot, like most race riots, was the result of longstanding
discrimination in jobs and housing, police brutality, and
historic and virulent racist treatment of black people since the
late 19th century. Detroit had been a hotbed of KKK activity
since the 1920s. As whites attacked blacks, blacks struck back
with equal vengeance. White gangs invaded Paradise Valley, a
black commercial district in Detroit. The Mayor asked
Roosevelt to send in Federal troops, who occupied the city for
six months. Twenty-five of the thirty-four people killed were

black, and of those, seventeen were killed by white policemen. As in the case of George W. Bush's indifference to the suffering of New Orleans residents during Katrina, Roosevelt refrained from making any statements against the white violence for fear of alienating his Southern constituencies, i.e., Dixiecrats.

In part iv: "there ain' no place fo' a po' ol' gal to go" is a line from Bessie Smith's famous "Backwater Blues," written in 1927.

about the author

Cheryl Clarke is a black lesbian feminist poet and author of four previous books of poetry: *Narratives: Poems in the Tradition of Black Women* (1982), *Living As a Lesbian* (1986), *Humid Pitch* (1989), *Experimental Love* (1993), and the chapbook, *Your Own Lovely Bosom* (2014). The critical study *After Mecca: Women Poets and the Black Arts Movement* and her collected work, *The Days of Good Looks: Prose and Poetry 1980-2005* were published in in 2005 and 2006 respectively. *Living As a Lesbian* was reprinted by Sinister Wisdom and Midsummer Night Presses as a Sapphic Classic. She co-edited with Steven G. Fullwood *To Be Left with the Body* (2008), a literary publication of the AIDS Project Los Angeles.

Her poetry, essays, and book reviews have appeared in numerous publications since 1979, including *Adrienne: A Poetry Journal of Queer Women*; *African American Literary Review*; *The Black Scholar*; *Callaloo: A Journal of African AmericanArts and Letters*; *Conditions*; *Kaylani Magazine*; *The Kenyon Review*; *Sinister Wisdom*, and anthologies including, *This Bridge Called My Back: Writing by Radical Women of Color*; *Home Girls: A Black Feminist Anthology*; *The World in Us: Lesbian and Gay Poetry of the Next Wave*; and *The Arc of Love: An Anthology of Lesbian Love Poems*.

She has served on the boards of New York Women Against Rape, New Jersey Women and AIDS Network, the Center for Lesbian and Gay Studies (New York City), and the Astraea Lesbian Foundation for Social Justice, among others. She received the David Kessler Award in 2013 from the Center for Lesbian and Gay Studies for her service to LGBT communities.

Since 2013, she has been a co-organizer of the annual Festival of Women Writers in Hobart, New York, the Book Village of the Catskills.

Visit her website cherylclarkepoet.com.

about the word works

The Word Works, a nonprofit literary organization, publishes contemporary poetry and presents public programs. The Hilary Tham Capital Collection publishes work by poets who volunteer for literary nonprofit organizations. Nomination forms are requested from qualifying nonprofits by April 15 and manuscript submissions from nominated poets by May 1. Other imprints include the Washington Prize, International Editions, and The Tenth Gate Prize. A reading period is also held in May.

Monthly, The Word Works offers free literary programs in the Chevy Chase, MD, Café Muse series, and each summer, it holds free poetry programs in Washington, D.C.'s Rock Creek Park. Annually in June, two high school students debut in the Joaquin Miller Poetry Series as winners of the Jacklyn Potter Young Poets Competition. Since 1974, Word Works programs have included: "In the Shadow of the Capitol," a symposium and archival project on the African American intellectual community in segregated Washington, D.C.; the Gunston Arts Center Poetry Series; the Poet Editor panel discussions at The Writer's Center; and Master Class workshops.

As a 501(c)3 organization, The Word Works has received awards from the National Endowment for the Arts, the National Endowment for the Humanities, the D.C. Commission on the Arts & Humanities, the Witter Bynner Foundation, Poets & Writers, The Writer's Center, Bell Atlantic, the David G. Taft Foundation, and others, including many generous private patrons.

An archive of artistic and administrative materials in the Washington Writing Archive is housed in the George Washington University Gelman Library. The Word Works is a member of the Council of Literary Magazines and Presses and its books are distributed by Small Press Distribution.

wordworksbooks.org

THE HILARY THAM CAPITAL COLLECTION

Mel Belin, *Flesh That Was Chrysalis*
Carrie Bennett, *The Landscape Is a Painted Thing*
Doris Brody, *Judging the Distance*
Sarah Browning, *Whiskey in the Garden of Eden*
Grace Cavalieri, *Pinecrest Rest Haven*
Christopher Conlon, *Gilbert and Garbo in Love*
    & Mary Falls: Requiem for Mrs. Surratt
Donna Denizé, *Broken like Job*
W. Perry Epes, *Nothing Happened*
Bernadette Geyer, *The Scabbard of Her Throat*
Barbara G. S. Hagerty, *Twinzilla*
James Hopkins, *Eight Pale Women*
Brandon Johnson, *Love's Skin*
Marilyn McCabe, *Perpetual Motion*
Judith McCombs, *The Habit of Fire*
James McEwen, *Snake Country*
Miles David Moore, *The Bears of Paris & Rollercoaster*
Kathi Morrison-Taylor, *By the Nest*
Tera Vale Ragan, *Reading the Ground*
Michael Shaffner, *The Good Opinion of Squirrels*
Maria Terrone, *The Bodies We Were Loaned*
Hilary Tham, *Bad Names for Women & Counting*
Barbara Louise Ungar, *Charlotte Brontë, You Ruined My Life*
    & Immortal Medusa
Jonathan Vaile, *Blue Cowboy*
Rosemary Winslow, *Green Bodies*
Michele Wolf, *Immersion*
Joe Zealberg, *Covalence*

THE TENTH GATE PRIZE

Jennifer Barber, *Works on Paper*, 2015
Lisa Sewell, *Impossible Object*, 2014

THE WASHINGTON PRIZE

Nathalie F. Anderson, *Following Fred Astaire*, 1998

Michael Atkinson, *One Hundred Children Waiting for a Train*, 2001

Molly Bashaw, *The Whole Field Still Moving Inside It*, 2013

Carrie Bennett, *biography of water*, 2004

Peter Blair, *Last Heat*, 1999

John Bradley, *Love-in-Idleness: The Poetry of Roberto Zingarello*, 1995, 2nd edition 2014

Christopher Bursk, *The Way Water Rubs Stone*, 1988

Richard Carr, *Ace*, 2008

Jamison Crabtree, *Rel[AM]ent*, 2014

Barbara Duffey, *Simple Machines*, 2015

B. K. Fischer, *St. Rage's Vault*, 2012

Linda Lee Harper, *Toward Desire*, 1995

Ann Rae Jonas, *A Diamond Is Hard But Not Tough*, 1997

Frannie Lindsay, *Mayweed*, 2009

Richard Lyons, *Fleur Carnivore*, 2005

Elaine Magarrell, *Blameless Lives*, 1991

Fred Marchant, *Tipping Point*, 1993, 2nd edition 2013

Ron Mohring, *Survivable World*, 2003

Barbara Moore, *Farewell to the Body*, 1990

Brad Richard, *Motion Studies*, 2010

Jay Rogoff, *The Cutoff*, 1994

Prartho Sereno, *Call from Paris*, 2007, 2nd edition 2013

Enid Shomer, *Stalking the Florida Panther*, 1987

John Surowiecki, *The Hat City After Men Stopped Wearing Hats*, 2006

Miles Waggener, *Phoenix Suites*, 2002

Charlotte Warren, *Gandhi's Lap*, 2000

Mike White, *How to Make a Bird with Two Hands*, 2011

Nancy White, *Sun, Moon, Salt*, 1992, 2nd edition 2010

George Young, *Spinoza's Mouse*, 1996

INTERNATIONAL EDITIONS

Kajal Ahmad (Alana Marie Levinson-LaBrosse, Mewan
    Nahro Said Sofi, and Darya Abdul-Karim Ali Najin,
    trans., with Barbara Goldberg), *Handful of Salt*
Keyne Cheshire (trans.), *Murder at Jagged Rock: A Tragedy*
    by Sophocles
Yoko Danno & James C. Hopkins, *The Blue Door*
Moshe Dor, Barbara Goldberg, Giora Leshem, eds.,
    The Stones Remember: Native Israeli Poets
Moshe Dor (Barbara Goldberg, trans.), *Scorched by the Sun*
Lee Sang (Myong-Hee Kim, trans.), *Crow's Eye View:*
    The Infamy of Lee Sang, Korean Poet
Vladimir Levchev (Henry Taylor, trans.), *Black Book of the*
    Endangered Species

ADDITIONAL TITLES

Karren L. Alenier, *Wandering on the Outside*
Karren L. Alenier & Miles David Moore, eds.,
    Winners: A Retrospective of the Washington Prize
Christopher Bursk, ed., *Cool Fire*
Barbara Goldberg, *Berta Broadfoot and Pepin the Short*
Frannie Lindsay, *If Mercy*
Marilyn McCabe, *Glass Factory*
Ayaz Pirani, *Happy You Are Here*
W.T. Pfefferle, *My Coolest Shirt*
Jacklyn Potter, Dwaine Rieves, Gary Stein, eds.,
    Cabin Fever: Poets at Joaquin Miller's Cabin
Robert Sargent, *Aspects of a Southern Story*
    & A Woman from Memphis
Nancy White, ed., *Word for Word*

www.ingramcontent.com/pod-product-compliance
Lightning Source LLC
Chambersburg PA
CBHW031004090426
42737CB00008B/680